From the Editor:

Thank you for purchasing *"Scrapbooking Beyond Your Imagination"*, A Guide to Creating Home Decor and Gifts Using Your Scrapbook Supplies. We have enjoyed producing another book for and by our customers. YOU, the creative scrapbooking artist are the talented people that give us ideas, send us submissions, buy our publications and encourage other creators to be inspired by our idea books. To you, we are grateful.

Creative Concepts is proud of this, our fifth idea book. *"Scrapbooking Beyond Your Imagination"* is not your ordinary idea book. The purpose of this book is to show different projects and gifts that can be created using your scrapbooking supplies. We hope this book will spark your imagination and encourage you to step out of your "usual" scrapbooking to create wonderful designs for your home, gifts and holidays.

Designed to help you showcase your creativity, *"Scrapbooking Beyond Your Imagination"* is full of ideas. We have included tips and techniques as well as ideas and examples from our many talented designers, the "Creative Concepts Creators". Whether you're a beginning scrapbooker or a seasoned crafter, "Scrapbooking Beyond Your Imagination" will be a valuable resource of inspiration intended to set your imaginations to work, defining, personalizing and expanding on the projects included within its pages.

Creative Concepts is blessed to be in this industry. *"Scrapbooking Beyond Your Imagination"*, like our other publications, has been a blessing from God for which we are truly thankful. God gave us many gifts, one of which is our imagination. With this imagination, He also gave us the ability to use it for our enjoyment. Our imaginations can lead us to places we would usually not go, and to ideas that surprise us. The old saying is true, "there is no limit to your imagination", so don't keep your imaginative creations hidden in scrapbooks. Channel your talents beyond the scrapbooks. We hope you use this book, with your imagination and talent to create memorable crafts for you, your family and your friends.

So, as the wheels begin to turn, look within these pages and begin to imagine the possibilities... a certain corner in your bedroom, that special gift for your Mom's birthday, a fun holiday accent - all made with the supplies you have. Don't be afraid to try a new technique or medium. As you begin to imagine the possibilities, your trip through the craft store will never be the same. You never know what may inspire your imagination to take you into new things. Just don't limit yourself to a piece of paper - go ***Scrapbook Beyond Your Imagination!***

Dena Crow
President/CEO
Creative Concepts

Scrapbooking

Credit Info:
Publisher :
Creative Concepts, Inc.
Editor:
Dena Crow
Senior Designer and Writer:
Leigh King
Photography and Graphic Design:
Roland Langley, Graphics South, Inc.

A special thank you is extended to all the many Creative Concepts Creators for contributing to the production of this book. Your talents are priceless and your encouragement is appreciated.

To Order, Please contact your local scrapbook store or:
Creative Concepts
Phone # 256-350-9994
Fax# 256-350-9939
Website: www.Scrapbookingideas.com
Email: CreativeConcepts@Scrapbookingideas.com

Vacation Mini Canvases
by Sue Kelemen of St. Louis, MO
Supplies:
3 4x4" Canvas: Canvas Concepts
Vacation Paper: K & Company
Embellishments: K & Company
Paint: Making Memories
Fibers: EK Adornments
Ribbon: May Arts
Ink: Tim Holtz

TIP
I painted the canvases green, then added the torn paper, photos and embellishments. I added the hanging hardware and accented with fibers and ribbons.

Wall decor can include not only scrapbooking pages, but also canvas art, clocks, frames and chalkboards. Most any project can be attached to a wall in some way. Don't keep your creativity hidden in a scrapbook. Display your artwork on a wall for others to enjoy. Imagine your projects displayed in your home, office or even a camper. So have fun, and add a personal touch to your walls with some of your personal creations!

Additional Supplies You May Need:
Canvas
Wall hanging hardware
Acrylic Paint

A Day at the Beach

by Leigh King of Decatur, AL

Supplies:
Paper: Daisy D's, Bazzill
Ribbon: Doodlebug Design
Letters: Making Memories, EK Success, Paperbilities
Stickers: Making Memories
Embellishment: Li'l Davis
Mesh: Just Charming
Seashells: from the beach
Other: 12"x24" canvas, acrylic paints, wooden plaque, wooden monogram, crown molding

Simone

by Renee Williams of Rochester, NY

Supplies:
Paper: Basic Grey Motifica
Monogram: Microsoft Word
Rub Ons: Chatterbox
Slide Mount: Creative Paper Clay
Stamp: Stampabilities
Metallic rub Ons: Craft-T
Inks: Stampin Up, Fresco Chalk, Stampabilities
Papier Glass Finish: Plaid

TIP

To make a paperclay slide mount: press the paper clay onto a slide mount. With damp fingers smooth the edges. Gently press the rubber stamp into two sides. Let dry overnight. Using your finger gently rub metallic rub ons to coordinate with paper Sand any rough edges inside or out. Finish with Papier Glass finish in Antique to age the color and "pop" the rubber stamp impression.

Print on textured cardstock to give your photo a "painted" feel. Ink the edges of the monogram and pages to give definition to each element.

Kimi, Aimee & Calliope
by Carrie Gay of Albany, OR
Supplies:
Paint: Plaid
Ribbon: May Arts
Foam Corner and Alpha Stamps:
Making Memories
Patterned Paper: Chatterbox
Stencil Letter: Making Memories
Chalk: Colorbox
Cardstock: Bazzill
Wooden Tag: Chatterbox
Decorative Brads:
Making Memories
Assorted Silk Flowers
Metal Disc: Pebbles
Date Stamp
Canvas

Reversible Sign
by Jennifer Miller of Humble, TX
Supplies:
Paper and Stickers: Mustard Moon
Ribbon: May Arts
Bottle Cap: Mustard Moon
Silk Flower
Gemstone: Westrim
Mod Podge: Plaid
Ink: Ranger

IDEA
I use this as a wall plaque in the study/scrap room. My husband and I joke how it is his study and I say it is my scrap room. One side says Jen's Scrap-room and the reverse says Lance's study.

Wall Flowers

by Amy Alvis of Indianapolis, IN

Supplies:

Little Princess:
Pattern Paper and Stickers: American Crafts
Mini Brad and Rub ons: Doodlebug, KI Memories
Metal Rimmed Tags and Rub Ons: Making Memories

Oh So Serious:
Rub Ons: Doodlebug
Patterned Paper: Paper Fever
Cardstock: Bazzill
Font: Goofball

Love Blossoms:
Patterned Paper and Tab: SEI
Rub Ons: Doodlebug
Tabs: KI Memories
Eyelets: Happy Hammer
Date Stamp: Making Memories

Baby Boy Wall Plaque

by Melanie Douthit of West Monroe, LA

Supplies:
Patterned Paper: Pebbles and Karen Foster
Cardstock: Bazzill
Stickers and Charm: Pebbles
Acrylic Paint: Apple Barrel and Folk Art
Crackle Finish: Delta Ceramcoat
Mod Podge: Plaid
Grosgrain Ribbon: unknown
Project created on a wooden plaque

TIP
Use adhesive backed foam mounting tape to give a raised 3-D appearance.

Wisdom Chalkboard
by Mackey Stanley of Conway, AR
Supplies:
Wooden Letters: Crafts Etc.
Patterned Paper: Basic Grey and Making Memories
Acrylic Paint: Delta and paint from my daughter's room
Acrylic Embellishments: Heidi Grace
Beads: Crafts Etc.
Pewter Plaque: Making Memories
Mate Sealer: Krylon

TIP
I sanded the entire board so the paint would adhere. The colors of paint and embellishments were chosen to match my daughter's room.

The Artist
by Mackey Stanley of Conway, AR
Supplies:
Paper: Basic Grey, Creative Imaginations, Scissors Sisters, 7Gygsies
Cardstock Stickers: Basic Grey
Embellishments: 7Gypsies, The Gallery, Making Memories
Adhesive: Zots by Therm O Web
Paint: Making Memories, Behr

TIP
I stripped everything off the back of the box and replaced with the papers listed, then dry brushed it with paints from my daughter's room. All of the artwork on the walls are miniatures of her artwork and photography that I photographed and printed onto canvas. I added her initial to the apron to make "hers." Everything in the box now represents a piece of my daughter, The Artist, whose photo is on the easel.

IDEA
I purchased the Shadow Box for a mere $3 on final clearance! The glass was broken, the easel was in pieces. All that really remained were two tubes of paint and the artist's apron. I knew exactly what to do with it!!

Moments in Time

by Sara McMartin of Richmond, VA

Supplies:
Canvas
Cork Tiles
Watch Face and parts
Patterned Paper and Cardstock: KI Memories
Letters, Ribbons and Rub Ons: KI Memories
Silk Flowers

A

by Tara Daigle of Baton Rouge, LA

Supplies:
Wooden Letter
Acrylic Paint: Plaid
Patterned Paper: Anna Griffin
Ink: 7 Gypsies
Ribbon: Offray

IDEA

Letters can be used as wall decor to decorate a room. You can use one letter as a initial or several to spell a word, for example a child's name, "play room" or the word "create" to inspire your imagination!

Wendy

by Pam Bumbaca of Litchfield, NH

Supplies:
Patterned Paper: Creative Imaginations
Paint, Alpha Letters, Rub Ons: Making Memories
Silk Flowers
Ribbons: Offray, Lil Davis, May Arts
Clipboard Circles and Boshers: Bazzill
Trim: Fibers By The Yard
Bottlecap: unknown
Mini File Folder: made from an index card
Mini Roladex Card: unknown
Staples

Clipboards can be used for a variety of purposes. Imagine all the possibilities! You can decorate with them on a wall, lay them on a table or desk, or display them in a special place. You can give them as gifts or adhere a magnet to the back to place on the refrigerator. Clipboards can be used as decoration or for practical purposes as a reminder or note board.

Love Clipboard

by Jeanne Wynhoff of Connell, WA

Supplies:
Mini Clipboard: Office Supply
Patterned Paper: Debbie Mumm
Bottlecaps: Unknown Source
Ribbon and Fibers: Fibers by the Yard
Love Jewels: Gartner Studios
Paper Clip & Staples: Office Supply
Button: Dress It Up
Cork Nameplate: Lazer Letterz
Acrylic Heart: Lazer Letterz
Love Stickers: Pebbles Inc
Dome Stickers: Marcella by K
Rub On Letters: Chatterbox
Word Stickers: Bo-Bunny Press, Pebbles
Cardstock: Bazzill
Circle Punch: EK Success
Rub on Words: Paper Bliss
Metal Word: Making Memories
Paint: Krylon
Silk Flower
Ink: StazOn, Memories
Key Charms: Unknown

Our Family

by Susan Stringfellow of Cypress, TX

Supplies:
6 x 9" Clipboard: Office Depot
Patterned Paper: 7 Gypsies
Vintage Images: Altered Pages
Cork "S": Lazer Letterz
Acrylic Definition Sticker: Lazer Letterz
Heart Stamp: Stampin Up
Letter Stamps and Ornamental Stamp: Making Memories
"remember when" Sticker: Autumn Leaves
Ribbons, Ric Rac, and Lace: Fibers by the Yard
Heart Mini Brads: Accent Depot
Permanent Adhesive Runner: Scrapbook Adhesives
Acrylic Paints: Plaid
Mod Podge Matte: Plaid
Ink: Black Pearl Ex

TIP

I like to change the photos on the clipboard to keep a new family picture displayed.

Sweet Talker

by Michaela Young-Mitchell of Safford, AZ

Supplies
Clipboard: Wal Mart
Patterned Paper and Stickers: Fancy Pants Designs
Ribbon: Offray, May Arts, Wright's
Ric Rac: Wrights
Pen: Zig by EK Success

Clipboard

by Carrie Gay of Albany, OR

Supplies
Paint: Delta
Patterned Paper: Chatterbox
Modge Podge
Silk Flowers
Glue Dots
Ribbons: May Arts
Silver Pill Box
Mini Brads: Lasting Impressions
Foam Corner Stamp, Rub Ons: Making Memories
Alpha stickers: Memories
Foam Tape
Stencils: Making Memories - Jigsaw

C Clipboard

by Carolyn Lontin of Highland Ranch, CO

Supplies:
Clipboard
Paper: Chatterbox
Library Cards
Chipboard Flowers: Heidi
Silk Flower, Brad: Making Memories
C Monogram: My Mind's Eye
Ribbon: May Arts
Rub Ons: Doodlebug, Scrapworks, Wordsworth
Stickers: American Crafts, Creative Imagination
Clip: Karen Foster

Family Recipes

by Jeanne Wynhoff of Connell, WA

Supplies:
Ribbon: Fibers by the Yard
Patterned Papers, Stickers: SEI
Alphabet Stickers: me & my BIG ideas
Letter Stickers: Sticker Studio
Stenciled R: Colorbox Fluid Chalk Ink
Ribbon Charm: Making Memories
Circle Punch: EK Success
Paint: Krylon
Staples: Office Supply

TIP

A fully functional clipboard, just slip your recipe cards under the clip.

Cory's Homework

by Leigh King of Decatur, AL

Paper: Bo-Bunny, Karen Foster, Bazzill
Stickers: Bo-Bunny
Stamp: Hero Arts
Accessories: Junkitz, Karen Foster, My Mind's Eye
Ribbon: May Arts
Acrylic Paint

Silver Magnets

by Wendy Woodby of Dover, AR

Supplies:

Glass slides: (I had some cut from my local glass house, 2 inches by 2 inches)
Microscope Slides
Aluminum Tape (hardware section of your local discount store)
Ribbons
Charms
Safety Pins
Wire
Decorative Paper
Silk Flowers
Die Cut Letters

IDEA

Using a square punch to make the opening, I simply attached a photo from behind. This is an excellent gift for Mother's Day, Grandparent's Day or just a reminder on one's own fridge! These make great magnets, nametags, gift bag accents, Christmas ornaments, pins, etc.

Magnets are great to use in many places. Don't just think of magnets on the refrigerator, file cabinets or dishwashers. Magnets are small frames. They can be used as decorative items, gift items or personal accessories. Think of the small little "spot" in your home where you need a personal touch or an extra embellishment on a wrapped gift. Use a magnet! Magnets can be hung a variety of ways. Self Adhesive magnetic strips can be mounted on the back of any small item and displayed anywhere. If the display area moves (i.e. a drawer or a cabinet door) you may want to use Velcro. If you are using it as a personal accessory, adhere a pin to the back so that it can be worn on a shirt or jacket. Just **imagine** the possibilities!

Mickey Magnet
by Leigh King of Decatur, AL
Supplies:
Paper: Bazzill, Chatterbox
Stickers: EK Success
Ribbon: May Arts
Twine
Office Clip
Acrylic Frame

Mickey Frame
by Leigh King of Decatur, AL
Monogram: Go West Studio
Paper Frame: My Mind's Eye
Paper: Basic Grey, Scrap-Ease
Ribbon: May Arts
Acrylic Frame

Recipe Crate

by Leigh King of Decatur, AL

Supplies:

Paper: Bo-Bunny, Karen Foster, Daisy D's, Bazzill

Stickers: Jolee's Boutique, me & my BIG ideas,

Ribbon: May Arts, Offray

Stamps: Hero Arts, EK Success

Embellishments: Paperbilities, Making Memories, Lasting Impressions, Foof-a-La

Other: wooden crate, acrylic paint, antiquing medium, decoupage, label maker

Home decor - what a great place to show off our talent, creativity and imagination! How we decorate our homes tells so much about us. Paper and embellishments can be found to complement any style in any room. You can find accessories to alter in flea markets and yard sales, new or unfinished at a gift or craft store, even sitting in your home in the corner or garage. You can start with the piece and imagine how it can be redecorated or get an idea, maybe from one featured here, and search out the piece you need to complete it. Whatever the case, don't be afraid to try something new. You may already have most, if not all, of the tools you need.

Additional Supplies You May Need:

All-purpose sealer
Acrylic paint
Decoupage medium
Strong paper adhesive

HOME DECOR

SECTION DIVIDERS

RECIPE CARDS

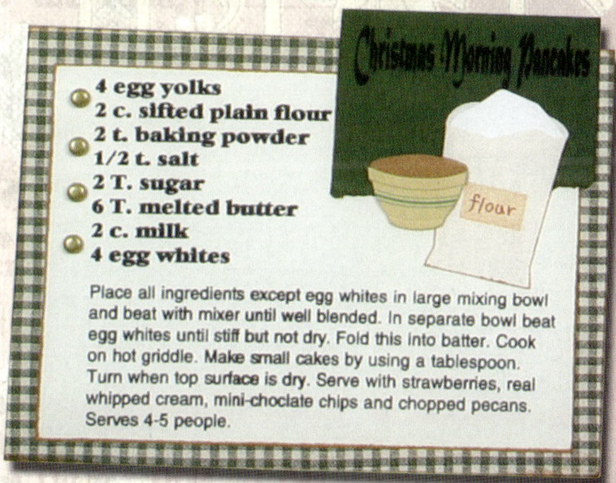

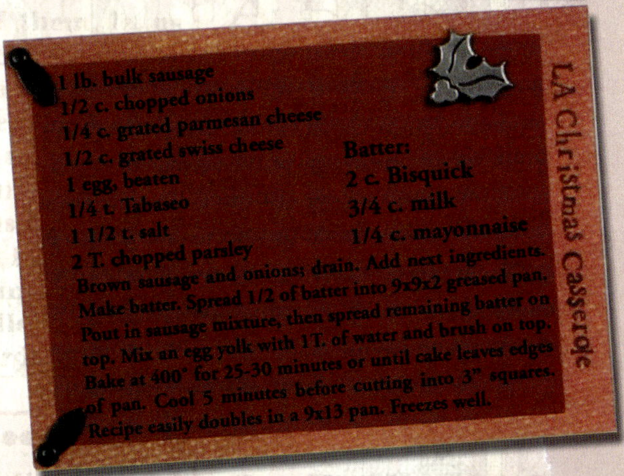

School Cork Board
by Leigh King of Decatur, AL
Supplies;
Paper: Foof-a-La
Stickers: Foof-a-La, Bo-Bunny
Ribbon: Offray
Cork Board

Tray
by Leigh King of Decatur, AL
Supplies;
Paper: Daisy D's
Fibers: Basic Grey
Wooden Tray
Silk Flower
Acrylic Paint
Decoupage

Love Candle

by Jeanne Wynhoff of Connell, WA

Supplies:
Ribbon: Fibers by the Yard
Velvet: Unknown
Faux Candy: Michael's
Ink: Colorbox Fluid Chalk
Sticker: All My Memories

Summertime Vase

by Sherry Wright of West Branch, MI

Supplies:
Paper: KI
Bottle Caps: Li'l Davis
Ribbon and Trim: me & my BIG ideas

Decorative Dress Form

by Leigh King of Decatur, AL

Supplies:
Stamps: Hero Arts, Judikins, Tin Can Mail, Making Memories
Stickers: Nostalgiques
Ephemera: me & my BIG ideas
Fibers: Magic Scraps
Other: paper mache' dress form, acrylic paint, decoupage, brass candlestick, mulberry paper

IDEA
What a great home accessory to add to a dressor, desk or your own special place.

Spring Birdhouse
by Leigh King of Decatur, AL
Supplies:
Paper, Stickers and Frame: K & Company
Stamp: Stampin' Up
Other: acrylic paint, decoupage

Tools of the Trade
by Leigh King of Decatur, AL
Paper, Brads: Karen Foster
Stickers: Frances Meyer
Paint Can
Ribbon
Washer
Picture Hanger
Distressing Ink

Calliope's Barrettes
by Carrie Gay of Albany, OR
Supplies:
Paint Can
Patterned Paper: Chatterbox
Adhesive: Alenes Tacky Glue
Ribbon: May Arts
Staples
Brads
Silk Flowers
Label: Dymo

Decorative Bucket

by Raechelle Bellus
of Spokane Valley, WA

Supplies:
Paper: Fancy Pants Designs
Eyelets: Making Memories
Ribbon: Offray
Ink: VersaMagic
Paint: Plaid

Spring Vase

by Sherry Wright
of West Branch, MI

Paper Mache Wastebasket: Walnut Hollow
Paper, Die Cuts, Stickers: K & Company
Silk Flowers
Trim: Wright's
Adhesive: Ther-O-Web Zots
Mod Podge: Plaid

Vintage Memories Photos

by Susan Stringfellow of Cypress, TX

Supplies:
Archival Photo File: SEI
Patterned and Velveteen Papers: Grannys Kitchen SEI
Ric Rac: Fibers by the Yard
Rhinestone Brads, Rub on Words, Stickers, and Page Tabs: SEI
Flower Trim: Fibers by the Yard
Number Stamps: Rubber Stamp Ave
Chestnut Roan Chalk Ink: Colorbox
Adhesive Tape: Scrapbook Adhesives
Diamond Glaze Adhesive: Judikins

Kiss Frame
by Melissa Kelley of Pueblo, CO
Supplies:
Patterned Paper: Paper Studio
Rubber Stamps: Leave Memories
Rubber Stamp Ink: StazOn by Tsukineko
Lace
Silk Flower
Metal Corner
Moulding
Safety Pin: Making Memories
Paint: Plaid

Frames are a natural extension of our scrapbook pages and there are many options available to be used: unfinished wood, acrylic, paperboard, papermache, etc. One of the great benefits is being able to use 3-D objects and accessories that would otherwise be too bulky within the confines of our scrapbooks. As you look at these examples, imagine how you can personalize your frame to fit your decor, your subject or your mood. Embellish it with coordinating accents, ribbon, souvenirs and memorabilia.

Additional Supplies You May Need:
All purpose sealer
Acrylic Paint
Antique Medium
Distressing Ink
Strong Craft Glue

Florida

by Andrea Cloutier of Boca Raton, FL
Supplies:
Frame: Savage Paper Easel Mat
Mesh: Magic Mesh
Paint: Making Memories
Sand: Designer's Library
Beads: unknown
Stamps: Stampin' Up!
Paper: Stampin' Up!
Embossing Powder: Powder Keg
Modeling Paste: Liquitex
Lettering Template: Pagerz

Dad Frame

by Jennifer Miller of Humble, TX
Supplies:
Paper: Mustard Moon
Mod Page: Plaid Ind.
Ribbon, Button, Letters: unknown

San Francisco Frame

by Elizabeth Lee of Monterey Park, CA
Supplies:
Cardstock: Bazzil
Patterned Paper: 7 Gypsies
Ribbon: May Arts
Stamp: Purple Onion
Chipboard Word: Li'l Davis
Silk Flower
Mini Tags and Definition Stickers: Making Memories
Postcard Sticker: unknown

Wooden Frame

by Sue Kelemen of St. Louis, MO

Supplies:
Wooden Frame: Provo Craft
Paper: Deja View
Ribbon: May Arts
Rubber Stamp Letters: PSX
Rubber Stamp Label: EK Success
Button: EK Success
Paint: Apple Barrell
Stamp Ink: Stazon, Tim Holtz

Together

by Leigh King of Decatur, AL

Supplies:
Paper: Daisy D's
Accessories: Lil' Davis Designs, Basic Grey, Making Memories
Wood Frame
Acrylic Paint
Decoupage

Hinged Canvas Book

by Sue Kelemen of St. Louis, MO

Supplies:
Two 6x6 Canvas: Canvas Concepts
Leather Frame: Making Memories
Ribbon: May Arts
Hinges: Karen Foster
Paint: Making Memories
Inside:
Paper: Tim Holtz
Bottle Cap: Design Originals
Clip: Tim Holtz
Large Slide Mount: Design Originals
Square Glass Slide: Tim Holtz
Key: K & Company
Metal Tape: Karen Foster
Brad: Karen Foster
Foam Mounting Tape
Rubber Stamp Clock: Santa Rosa
Distress Ink: Tim Holtz

TIP

Painting can be added to almost any project and the tips and techniques are numerous. These tips will help you get started if you want to make a project with wood or paper mache.

Painting: Your piece will accept paint better if you first apply an all-purpose sealer, found in the craft store near the acrylic paint. If wood, sand the piece lightly before and after applying sealer with a fine grade paper or sanding sponge. Remove any dust. Paint the piece with acrylic paint, using smooth even strokes. May need a second coat.

For a stained effect, follow the above directions, but wipe off the excess paint as you go. Acrylic paint dries quickly, so work one small area at a time. This will give you the color you want, but allow some of the grain to show through.

A distressed look really adds a lot of interest to your piece. Follow the above instructions for either look. When your paint is dry, apply an antiquing medium, following the instructions on the bottle. You may choose to sand off some areas before applying the antique medium or apply an off-white, using a dry brush technique. This will give it the look of being well loved without all the work. Refer to an example of this technique on page 20. *the recipe box*

Oh Boy Frame

by Sabrina Gould of Melbourne, FL

Supplies:
Paper: SEI
Ink: Ranger
Cardstock Stickers: SEI
Pop Dots: All Night Media
Adhesive: Krylon, Scotch

TIP

I Sprinkled baby powder on the back of the cardstock stickers so that they would not be sticky when I placed pop dots on them to make them three-dimensional.

TIP

The frame was created using a 3-part platform box by Grassroots Design. I took the box insert, sewed a clear pocket on the front from a page protector. Then I attached it to one side of the box so it "hinges" open. I printed out several photos and matted them to a size to fit in the pocket. I put one in the pocket and the rest are stored in the space underneath. The ribbon tab is velcroed into place so it stays shut while the "frame" is upright. Then I decorated with paint, rub-ons and a handmade fabric heart. It will sit on my mom's desk like a regular photo frame but she can open it, select a new photo and slide it in whenever she feels like it!

Memories Frame

by Melissa Kelley of Pueblo, CO

Supplies:
Patterned Paper: Unknown
Platform Box: Grassroots Design
Rub ons: Making Memories
Ribbon: May Arts
Paint: Plaid
Fabric Heart: my own design

Sweet Slumber

by Melanie Douthit of West Monroe, LA

Supplies:
Patterned Paper: Chatterbox
Cardstock: Bazzill Basics
Vellum Quote: Flair Designs, Inc.
Flowers: Making Memories
Brads: Creative Impressions
Ink: Colorbox Fluid Chalk Ink
Paint and Crackle Finish: Delta Ceramcoat

Beauty Frame
by Maegan Hall of Virginia Beach, VA
Supplies:
Paper: Chatterbox
Flower: Jolee's Boutique
My own handwriting

Girl's Peg Rack
by Melissa Kelley of Pueblo, CO
Supplies:
Patterned Paper: K & Co
Ribbon: Offray
Stickers: EK Success
Rubber Stamps: Leave Memories
Rubber Stamp Ink: Clearsnap
Silk Flowers
Paper Flowers: Making Memories
Buttons: Crafts Etc.
Paint: Plaid
Wood Plaque and Pegs

Summer and the Living is Easy

by Teresa Bean of Tampa, FL
Supplies:
Stickers: Susan Branch
Green Glass Beads: Fire Mountain
Shells, Twig, Sand, Cardstock, Mulberry: Remember When
Mesh, Fish Charm: Handmade

TIP
The shells were collected from the beach and the "drift wood" is cypress mulch from my garden.

Dog Sign

by Teresa Bean of Tampa, FL
Supplies:
Recycled CD
Stickers, Spiral Clip: Making Memories
Buttons: Jessie James
Bone Punches: EK Success
Shake Box: Paper Bliss
Cut Outs: Fiber By the Yard
Mini Clothes Pins: Card Connection
Mulberry, Cardstock: Remember When
Paw Print Stickers: Provo Craft
Glaze: Judikins
Gold Typewriter Keys: Scraps-N-More
Ribbon: Offray
Paint: Plaid
Assorted Beads and Seeds

If you love trash to treasure projects, this idea is for you. There is no end to the possibilities of what you can do with a decorated CD; as a clock, a picture frame, an element on another decorated item, a unique greeting card, in a set as wall decor. However you imagine it, it's bound to be one-of-a-kind and totally reflective of your distinctive style.

Additional Supplies You May Need:
Decoupage medium
Strong paper adhesive

CD Art
by Teresa Bean of Tampa, FL
Supplies:
Recycled CD
Fibers: Fiber By The Yard
Glass Pebbles
Paper Rose: Card Connection
Paper: Sonnets
Mulberry: Remember When
Collage Images: unknown
Glass Bugle Beads: Fire Mountain Gems

TIP
Each glass bugle bead was glued around the edge of the CD using tweezers. It creates a beautiful shiny edging to the finished CD.

Time
by Mackey Stanley of Conway, AR
Supplies:
Cardstock, Stickers: Sandylion
Adhesive: Krylon
Paint: Making Memories
CD

IDEA
The clock parts fit perfectly inside the hole of the CD so no further drilling is required.

Miller Recipes
by Jennifer Miller of Humble, TX
Supplies:
Wood Box: Darice
Patterned Paper, Stencil: Rusty Pickle
Rub Ons: Rusty Pickle, Chatterbox
Brad: Bazzill
Flower: unknown
Mod Podge: Plaid

Decorative boxes offer us an opportunity to make storage beautiful. What better way to store photos, memorabilia, a special gift, craft or cosmetic supplies. Like Home Decor, a box can be embellished to fit any room or season. Use them to hold precious baby memories, wedding or holiday mementos or just to keep unsightly clutter contained. Boxes can be found in craft stores or basements, made of wood or paper mache, new or previously owned and loved. No matter how you choose to use it your decorated box will brighten a room every time it's used.

Additional Supplies You May Need:
All-purpose sealer
Acrylic paint
Decoupage medium
Strong paper adhesive

Leaving Prints On My Heart

by Gwen Dye of Enterprise, AL

Supplies:
Acrylic Paint: Delta
Paper: K & Company, Anna Griffin
Rub Ons: (bears) Provo Craft
Circle Tag
Various Stamps (heart, footprints and alphabet)
Ribbon: Offray
Distress Ink: Ranger
Eyelets

IDEA

The Memory Box Artist Program, Inc (www.memory-boxes.org) is an organization which "provides boxes for families of infants that pass away in the hospital so that the families did not leave the hospital empty handed without any representation of that child's life."

Initial Box

by Jennifer Miller of Humble, TX

Supplies:
Wood Box: Darice
Patterned Paper: Mustard Moon
Stickers: Mustard Moon
Mod Podge: Plaid

School Days Box
by Leigh King of Decatur, AL
Supplies:
Paper: Karen Foster, Bazzill
Stickers: me & my BIG ideas, Karen Foster, EK Success
Embellishments: All My Memories, Karen Foster, Lasting Impressions
Ribbon: May Arts
Pencil Box
Book Plate

Travel Box
by Tara Daigle of Baton Rouge, LA
Supplies:
Pencil Box
Paper: Paper Love Designs
Ink: Colorbox Fluid Chalk
Letter Stickers: Jolee's
Letters: Scrabble Game
Magic Mesh

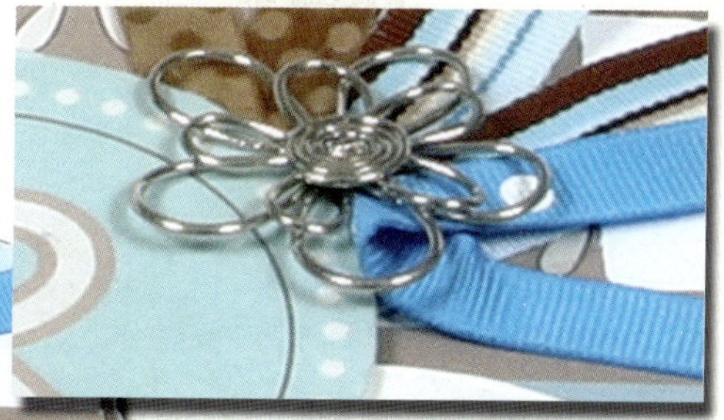

Chris' Box

by Pam Bumbaca of Litchfield, NH

Supplies:
Made from a wooden box bought at Craft/Hobby Store
Acrylic Paint
Papers and Coasters: SEI
Ribbon
Boshers: Bazzill
Metals: Making Memories, Karen Foster
Silk Flowers
Ink: Close To My Heart
Trim: Fibers By the Yard
Leather Frame: Making Memories

Tags are placed inside the gift box.

Scrapbook Emergency Kit
by Susan Stringfellow of Cypress, TX
Supplies:
Paper Mache Box: MSI
Patterned Papers: SEI
Stickers: SEI
Scrappers Sanding Block: PM Designs
Black Stazon Ink: Tsukineko
Small Letter and Dragonfly Stamps: Hero Arts
Larger Letter Stamps: Rubber Stamp Ave
Fibers: Fibers by the yard
Other: Transparency, Rhinestone Stud, Adhesive, Foam Tape
Small scrapping embellishments inside box lid shadowbox

IDEA
What a great gift for a scrapbooking friend! Include some of her favorite embellishments and she is sure to have an "emergency."

Tools & Things
by Kathleen Summers of Roseville, CA
Supplies:
Mini Lunch Box: Provo Craft
Patterned Paper: Making Memories
Ribbon: Heidi Swapp
Wood Frame: Chatterbox
Rub On Letters: Making Memories
Foam Letter Stamps: Li'l Davis Designs
Ink: Tsukineko

IDEA
Alter a mini lunchbox for holding scrapbooking tools.

Love Box
by Jeanne Wynhoff of Connell WA
Supplies:
Paint: Plaid
Patterned Paper: Reminisce
Stickers: Reminisce
Ribbon and Ric-Rac: Fibers By the Yard
Ink: Colorbox Fluid Chalk Ink
Mini Brad: Eyelet Outlet
Flower: Craft Store
Crystal Lacquer

Memories
by Leigh King of Decatur, AL
Paper: me & my BIG ideas
Accessories: Making Memories
Ribbon: SEI
Paper Mache' Box
Alphabet Stamps: Hero Arts
Decoupage
Acrylic Paint

Jewelry Box
by Leigh King of Decatur, AL
Supplies:
Stickers: Nostalgiques by EK Success
Stamps: Stampabilities
Quote: ColorOasis by EK Success
Acrylic Paint
Decoupage Medium
Printed Paper: Autumn Leaves

Jewelry Box
by Leigh King of Decatur, AL
Paper: Creative Imaginations
Paper Mache' Box
Wooden "feet"
Beads
Acrylic Paint
Decoupage

Boxes of Love
by Raechelle Bellus
of Spokane Valley, WA
Supplies:
Paper: KI
Ribbon: unknown
Paper Mache Boxes

Heritage Treasure Box
by Sue Kelemen of St. Louis, MO
Supplies:
Box -
Unfinished Wooden Cigar Box: Darice
Paper: 7 Gypsies, Design Originals, K & Company
3D Frame: K & Company
Ruler Frame and Tag: Grand Adhesions
Tiny Metal Frame: K & Company
Paints: Apple Barrel, Making Memories
Ribbons: May Arts
Brads: All My Memories
Black Cardstock: Bazzill

Mini Album -
Paper: EK Success
Scroll: Design Originals
Bookbinding Tape: Making Memories
Adhesive Tabs: Rusty Pickle
Ribbon: K & Company
String Clasps: K & Company

TIP
I bent the license plate to give it more of a beat up look. I used screw brads in the plate holes.

Vacation Memories Box
by Sue Kelemen of St. Louis, MO
Supplies:
Wooden Cigar Box: Darice
Off White Paint
Rubber Stamps: unknown
Letter Stamps: Creative Imagination
Clear Embossing Powder
Foam Letter Stamps: Making Memories
Bottle Caps: Design Originals
Cardboard Circles: Bazzill Chips

Inside Box -
Paper: Karen Foster
Stickers: Karen Foster

Accordion Mini Album -
Paper: Science Route
Slide Mounts
Stickers: Karen Foster
Fibers: EK Success
Ribbons: May Arts
Brads: Boxer
Memories Stamp: EK Success
Staples: Making Memories

Blue Decorative Box
by Raechelle Bellus of Spokane Valley, WA
Supplies:
An old cigarette tin (10"x 4"x5")
Paper and Stickers: Arctic Frog
Machine Stitching

My Friend Box
by Cindy Harris of Modesto, CA
Supplies:
Patterned Paper: Pebbles
Stickers: Pebbles
Ribbon: Offray
Black Photo Corners: 3L
Foam Tape: 3M
Paint: Making Memories
Scissors and Paper Trimmer: EK Success
Chalk: Craft-T
Double Sided Tape: Art Accents

Mac's Purse

by Mackey Stanley of Conway, AR

Supplies:
Basswood Cigar Purse
Cardstock, Paper: Junkitz, Fontwerks
Rubber Stamps: Postmodern Design, Fontwerks Shapes
Ribbon: Flair Designs and Offray
Beads: Fimo Clay
Wooden Embellishments: Artistic
Fabric Pockets: Making Memories
Copper Tag: Heidi Grace Elements
Adhesive: Krylon Matte Sealant
Paint: Making Memories
Ink: Ancient Page

IDEA

Each element on the purse represents something about me ^ from my initial "M" to the mountain stamp - we live high on top a mountain. The words on the large wooden "M" express things that are important to me as well.

TIP

The majority of the coloring on the purse is actually done with pigment ink to give it a distressed finish. Everything has been sanded before and after it was added.

Imagine the response you'll get when you carry a beautifully adorned carry-all that you embellished from your scrapbooking supplies. Whether you add pictures of your grandchildren or a fabulous vacation, or use a monogram with your favorite papers and embellishments, it will reveal who you are and what you love. Of course, it will also make a fabulous gift either on its own or to carry a surprise within. You have several options to choose from including lunch boxes, cigar boxes or galvanized pails. Don't forget to adorn the handle with beads and ribbon, or whatever your unique project calls for.

Additional Supplies You May Need:
Purse handle
Decoupage medium
All-purpose sealer
Acrylic paint
Fabric or felt for lining

Mexico Purse

by Sue Kelemen of St. Louis, MO

Supplies:
Unfinished Wood Cigar Box with Purse Handle: Darice
Paper: Karen Foster, K & Company, Design Originals
Chipboard Letters: Li'l Davis
Letter and Number Stickers: Memories Complete
Twill Word Stickers: All My Memories
Month/Date License Plate Stickers: Stickers Studio
Metal Disc: Tim Holtz
Letter Stickers: Club Scrap
Paper: Club Scrap
Paint: Making Memories
Mica Chip: USArt Quest
Charms: unknown
Rub Ons: Chatterbox
Clear Epoxy Sticker Letters: Creative Imaginations
Ink: Ranger
Mod Podge
Scrappy Tape: Magic Scraps
Other: Coins, Sand

TIP
I found a children's book with a window cut out that fit just right into the box.

Pam's Cigar Purse

by Pam Bumbaca of Litchfield, NH

Supplies:
Cigar Box
Paper: K & Company
Purple "Paper": Velvet
Purse Handle
Ribbon
Metal Letters: Making Memories
Ribbon Slide: Adorned Pages
Pre-flattened Bottle Cap: unknown
Staples

Teacher Gift Set
by Cindy Harris of Modesto, CA
Pattern Paper, Stickers, Wooden Tags: Pebbles
Twine, Ties and Brad Frame: Pebbles
Ink: Staz-on
Ribbon: Offray
Foam Tape: 3M
Scissors, Paper Trimmer: EK Success
Tape: Art Accents
Other: Clipboard, Door Hanger, Box

As scrapbook artists we often want to share our talents as gifts for the special people in our lives, but creating a scrapbook can be very time consuming and costly. This section re-imagines those ideas into fabulous, do-able projects anyone can complete: matching gift sets, mini-albums and unique gift containers with matching cards. Again, the possibilities are endless. Miniature accordion folded "scrapbooks" can be designed around one idea or subject. Celebrate an occasion or accomplishment using a set of beautifully coordinated paper and embellishments widely available. Anyone would feel honored and special to receive such a personal gift from you.

Back to School

by Leigh King of Decatur, AL

Paper: Bo-Bunny, Karen Foster, Bazzill
Stickers: Bo-Bunny, Karen Foster, me & my BIG ideas, EK Success
Stamps: Hero Arts, Making Memories
Ribbons: May Arts, Basic Grey, Offray, SEI
Embellishments: Bazzill, Karen Foster, Making Memories
Distressing Ink
Label Maker
Key Tags
Alphabet Beads
Pencil

more →

IDEA

Don't limit your imagination by thinking all scrapbooks must be confined to an album. Explore the possibilities that fit within the theme of the book or project you're creating. There are many useful options and techniques.

The office supply store carries many useful items for binding. Paper fasteners, brads with washers, shaped paperclips, metal book rings and slide clips are a few ideas. Many stores also offer plastic or wire binding services which may prove a little more durable.

For a more industrial look try shopping in the hardware store. Chunky screws, washers and nuts, beaded chain or even a wooden dowel can be used to create a fun, masculine look to your special project.

A craft oriented look can be achieved with more traditional resources like ribbon and paper. Accordian folding is a popular method and further described on page 49. Book binding can be achieved by folding several pages together, creating a signature, that you can then tie around the spine to secure or sew in place. Just make sure to plan ahead for this type of binding as this may change the page order in your project.

School Days Album

by Margaret Winters of Wichita, KS

Supplies:
Vellum, Cardstock: Leaving Prints
Pencil Cut Out: Leaving Prints
Alphabet Stickers: Provo Craft
Computer Font: Problem Secretary
Ribbon: Offray

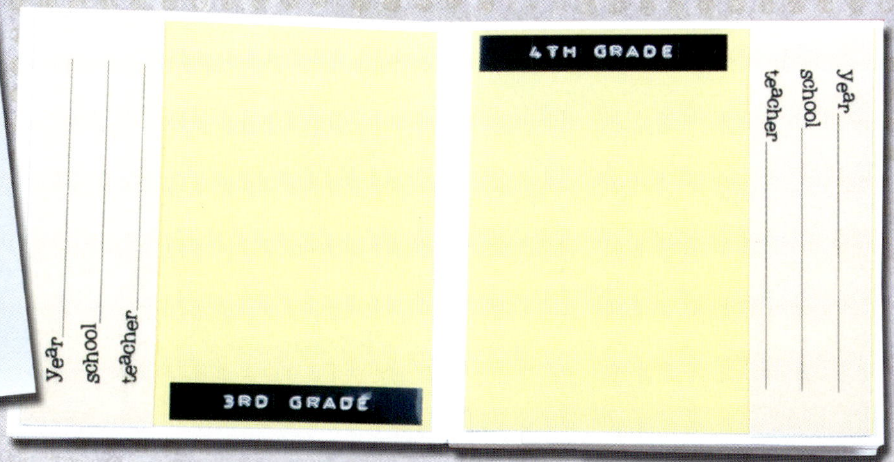

Childhood Treasure

by Sue Kelemen of St. Louis, MO
(CD Folder Mini Album)
Supplies:
Three Blank CD Holders
Paper, Die Cuts: Daisy D's
Clear Index Tab: Avery
Cotton Twill: 7 Gypsies, Creative Expressions
Brads: All My Memories
Date Stamp: Making Memories
Jump Rings: Junkitz
Silk Daisy

IDEA

Each Page will hold a 2.5"x 3.5" regular size wallet photo. These would be wonderful to give as a gift to a high school graduate, a preschool graduate or make one for your own child's room. They are easy to make. This one is small, a 4.5"x 4.5" size. They may also be made for 6"x 6".

Party Invitation and Gift Bag

by Margaret Winters of Wichita, KS
Supplies:
Cardstock: Making Memories
Patterned Paper: DieCuts With a View
Ribbon: Offray
Buttons: Dress It Up
Little Letter Stickers: Making Memories
Circle Punch: Marvy
Party Favor Box: Bought at the Dollar Tree Store

TIP

I printed the words in a circle using the Microsoft word program.

Happy Birthday Paint Can
from Catherine Allan of Twin Falls, ID
Supplies:
Cut Outs: All My Memories
Circle Punch and Scissors: Family Treasures
Letter Stencil: Office Max
Letter Beads: Westrim
Paint: Delta
Buttons: HillCreek, Making Memories, Magic Scraps
Ribbon: unknown
Fiber: Rub-a-Dub

Birthday Bucket
by Raechelle Bellus of Spokane Valley, WA
Supplies:
Paint Can: Ace Hardware
Patterned Paper: Fancy Pants Designs
Foam Stamps and Paint: Making Memories
Paint: Plaid
Ribbon: Offray
Machine Stitching
Ink: Versa Magic

Birthday Paper Bag Album
by Cindy Harris of Modesto, CA
Supplies:
Patterned Paper, Cut Outs: O' Scrap
Cardstock: Bazzill
Foam Tape: 3M
Rub Ons: Doodlebug
Scissors, Trimmer: EK Success
Ric Rac: Doodlebug
Double Sided Tape: Art Accents
Alphabet Stickers: SEI
Embroidery Floss: DMC
Ribbon: May Arts
Hole Punch: Karen Foster

Housewarming Gift Set
by Jennifer Miller of Humble, TX
Supplies:
Picture Frame -
Wood Frame: Provo Craft
Patterned Paper: Chatterbox
Soft Spoken Embellishments: me & my BIG ideas
Font: CAC
Modge Podge: Plaid Ind.
Key Box -
Wooden Box: Michaels
Patterned Paper: Chatterbox
Die Cut Tag, Flower, Lettering: Quickutz
Ribbon: May Arts
Brad: Creative Impressions
Modge Podge: Plaid Ind.
Card -
Patterned Paper: Chatterbox
Die Cut Tag: Quickutz
Ribbon: May Arts
Font: Scrap Mommy
Tag-
Patterned Paper: Chatterbox
Die Cut Tag: Quickutz
Ribbon: May Arts
Brad: Bazzil
Stamp: Close to My Heart
Ink: Stampin' Up

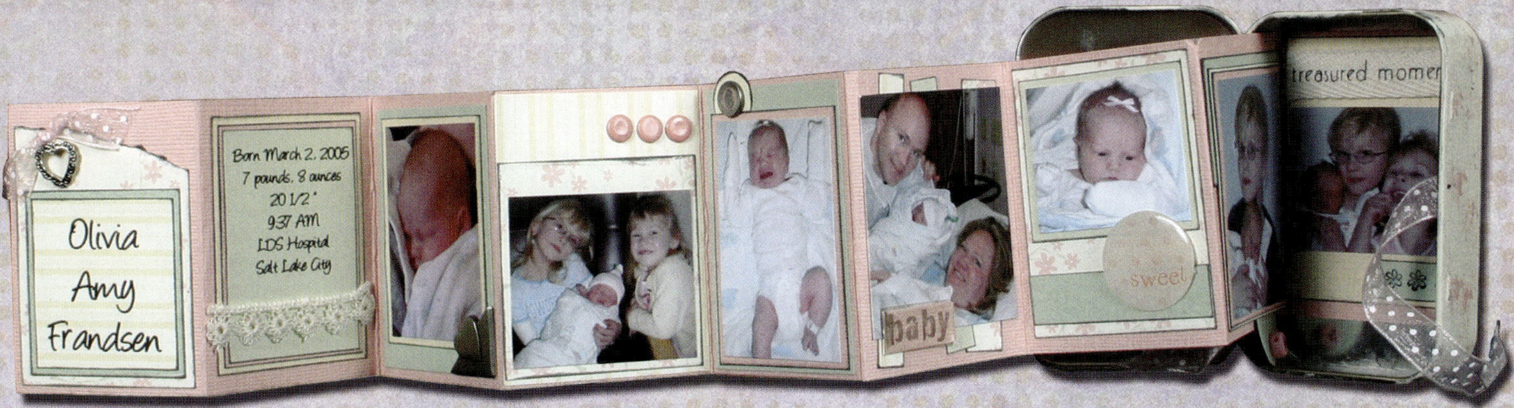

Baby Girl

by Catherine Allan of Twin Falls, ID

Supplies:
Patterned Paper: Chatterbox
Flowers, Snaps, Paint, Heart Corner Charm: Making Memories
Paint: Country Colors
Ribbon: May Arts
Heart charm: unknown
Epoxy Word: Creative Imaginations
Letter Bead: Westrim
Ink: ColorBox Charcoal Chalk
Letter Stamp: Hero Arts
Twill: Card Connection
Lace
Modge Podge

TIP

I accordion-folded cardstock measured to fit inside the tin, then decorated the "pages." The outside is painted and Mod-Podged.

Fun in the Sun Gift Album

by Susan Stringfellow of Cypress, TX

Supplies:
4x4" Yellow Gift Album: Die Cuts With a View
Yellow Cardstock: Die Cuts With a View
Paper: Doodlebug Designs
Cardstock Stickers & Dragonfly Token: Doodlebug Designs
Ribbon & Fluffy Fibers: Fibers By the Yard
Scrappers Block Sanding Block: PM Designs
Yellow Square Brads: unknown
Decorative Foam Stamp: Making Memories
White Acrylic Paint: Plaid
Permanent Adhesive: Scrapbook Adhesives
Stamp Letters: Hero Arts
Ink: Stampin' Up

American Soldier

by Margaret Winters of Wichita, KS

Supplies:
Cardstock: Making Memories and Leaving Prints
Pattern papers: NRN Design and K&Co. (LJ London Map)
Stickers: Sticker Studio (Freedom in the Retro Active collection)
Embossed Tags: Hot Off the Press
Ribbon: Offray
Ink Pad: ColorBox
Gold Metal Rimmed Tags and Mini Brads: JoAnn ScrapEssentials
Magnetic Stamp: Making Memories
Alphabet Stamps: EK Success
Transparencies: HammerMill
Square Punch: Creative Memories
Pen: Marvy Gel Excel
Fonts: Black Jack Regular, Safrole
Items from my craft supply

IDEA

I have always wanted to do a layout for my husband using the lyrics to Toby Keith's song titled "American Soldier". Instead I decided to make a small accordion album using the lyrics so I could give it to him as a gift.

Vacation Mini Book

by Sue Kelemen of St. Louis, MO

Supplies:

Paper, Die Cuts, Circles with Words: Club Scrap
Acrylic Frame: Heidi Grace
Ink: Versa Color
Bottle Cap: Design Originals
Charm: unknown
Happiness Sticker: EK Success
Fibers: EK Success
Brads: Boxer
Cardboard Circle: Bazzill Chip
Circle Punch: EK Success
Tag: Avery
Buckle: Making Memories
Letter Stamps: River City Rubber
Date Stamp: Making Memories

IDEA

Accordian folding can be used on your project in several different ways. Some of the more popular include: to add special interest as an embellishment, to allow more room for journaling or extra pictures, as binding on a project, as the project itself. With a little practice, the following instructions should help you achieve the look you desire.

The project itself:

To create an accordian folded project, first decide the size of your pages. For example, to make a 4x4" book with 14 front and back pages, you need a 12x12 piece of cardstock. Cut to make 3 - 4x12" strips. Use a bone folder or scoring tool to make mountain and valley folds, every 4 inches -- that's 1 mountain fold and 1 valley fold per strip. Stand up each strip and match the folds to make one long strip. As you glue together the end pages note that by putting the outside end page into the new strip's fold, your strip will look continuous with no edges showing.

Accordian folded binding:

The concept is the same as the above, only narrower and requiring more planning. Measure the heighth of your project and trim paper to that measurement. The width will depend on the number of pages in the book. You will again create the mountain and valley folds, scoring every 1/2". Careful measuring is required for the folds to turn out evenly. If you need more folds than your paper allowed, begin another fold, gluing in as in the above instructions. Attach the pages of your project to the mountain fold with a strong paper glue.

Refer to the index for specific projects within this book that used accordian folding.

Paper Bag Valentine

by Sue Kelemen of St. Louis, MO

Supplies:
Three Brown Paper Lunch Bags
Paper: 7 Gypsies, Rusty Pickle
Stickers: K & Company, Memories Complete, Making Memories, Wordsworth
Vellum quotes: Die Cuts With a View
Ribbon: May Arts, K & Company
Twist Ties: Club Scrap
Letter Stamps: Stampin' Up
Button: EK Success
Metal Clip, Safety Pin, Buckle: Making Memories
Love Quote: unknown
Adhesive Cork: Karen Foster
Vellum: unknown
Cardstock Tab: Heart and Home
Ink: Nick Bantok, Van Dyke
Charm: unknown

(back cover)

Thankful Accordion Album

by Margaret Winters of Wichita, KS

Supplies:
Cardstock: Bazzill and Making Memories
Patterned Papers: Chatterbox Great Room
Embellishments: Chatterbox
Mini Brads, Photo Anchors: Making Memories
Charms: Darice
Ribbon: Offray
Labeler: Dymo
Die Cuts: Sizzix
Pen: Zig Millennium
Ink: ColorBox
Ink Pad: Hero Arts Shadow
Alphabet Stickers: Provo Craft
Circle Punches: Creative Memories
Other items from my craft supply

IDEA

I really like the accordion albums to display an album entirely just by spreading the pages out. I plan on displaying this album across my fireplace mantel during the fall months. I want it to be something that I display yearly. I made several pockets throughout the book so I can forever add journaling when I want to. This book is to be used as a decorative home decor piece so that any friends and family visiting our home can view the book and the pictures inside it yet I did many hidden journaling tabs so that it gave the book the feel of being somewhat reclusive also.

Orca Address Book

by Susan Stringfellow of Cypress, TX

Supplies:
Cardstock: Bazzill
Textured Cardstock: Creative Imaginations
Patterned Papers: KI Memories
Orca Image: PM Designs
Fibers: Fibers By the Yard
Swirl Stamp: All Night Media
Letter Stamps: Rubber Stamp Avenue
Tiny Letter Stamps: Hero Arts
White Embossing Powder: Ranger
Black Pearl Ex ink: Jacquard Products
Black Mini Brads: Making Memories
Jewel Rivet: Michaels

Beautiful stationery says so much about someone -- and you have everything you need already at your fingertips as a scrapbooker. Pretty paper, stickers, stamps all add up to create thoughtful, decorative sentiments for you to send to the special people in your life. Imagine how special you would feel knowing someone took the time to make you such a personal gift. Stationery sets, personalized address books, specially adorned cards and journals are a pleasure to make and use ourselves as well as share with others -- for it is in the giving that we receive.

Additional Supplies You May Need:
Chipboard
Decoupage medium
Binder clasps or split rings
Composition notebook

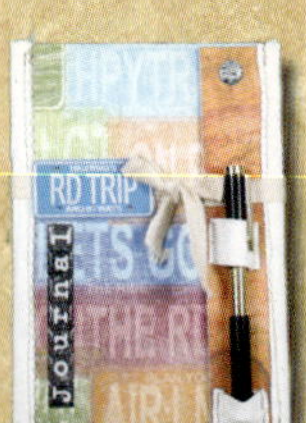

Monogrammed Stationary Book

by Leigh King of Decatur, AL

Supplies:
Paper: KI Memories, Bazzill
Monogram Letters: KI Memories
Charm: Karen Foster
Safety Pin, Vellum Tag: Making Memories
Fibers: Basic Grey
Ribbon: SEI
Other: Chipboard, Large White Envelopes, Binder Rings

IDEA

Store bought journals and composition notebooks are easily converted into treasured gifts and beautiful personal items. To begin select the paper and embellishments you wish to use. You can use a single sheet or several for a decoupage effect. Measure the front cover of the book, allowing an extra 1 1/2" in heighth and 3/4" in the width. For a softer look, tear edge of paper down the length of one side. If you plan on using distressing ink on the rest of your project, add it to the torn edge now. Lay over the top of the journal, torn edge to the spine, and crease the paper where it will wrap around the cover. Using a good book glue or decoupage medium, completely coat the back of your paper up to the crease lines and adhere to the journal cover, torn edge towards the spine. Carefully smooth out any air bubbles. Wrap your edges, miter the corners and adhere with your glue. Continue covering the back and inside covers for a completed look and embellish as desired.

Oriental Journal

by Teresa Bean of Tampa, FL

Supplies:
Metal Charms: Boxer Scrapbooks
Fibers: Fibers By the Yard
Papers: Fiskars
Glass Beads: Fire Mountain Gems
Rhinestones, Magazine Images, Mulberry: Remember When
Inks: Colorbox
Coin Sticker: Rebecca Sower
Slide Mailer: Scraps-n-More
Paint: Plaid

IDEA
The was created using a new slide mailer. They are meant to be used to mail glass specimen slides to labs for testing. I removed the center strip of cardboard to make a large niche for my pagoda image.

Dearest

by Jeanne Wynhoff of Connell, WA

Supplies:
Patterned Paper: Daisy D's
Punch Outs: Daisy D's
Rub-on Words: Provo Craft
Ribbon, Trim: Fibers By the Yard
Button: Dress It Up
Brad: Karen Foster
Staples: Office Supply
Magic Mesh
Ink: Colorbox Fluid Chalk Ink

Ramona
by Maegan Hall
of Virginia Beach, VA
Supplies:
Paper: Anna Griffin
Font: Bernard
Chipboard
Ribbon: Offray
Silk Flower
Brad: Making Memories
Cardstock: Bazzill
Tape: Thermo-Web

TIP
I cut the monogram R out of chipboard.

Memory Jar and Journal

by Angie Hagist of Jacksonville, FL

Supplies:
Patterned Paper: Chatterbox
Decorative Paper: Karen Russell Transparency
Cardstock: Bazzill Chatterbox
Ribbons/Fibers: May Arts, Unknown
Stickers: Chatterbox, Deluxe Designs, Rebecca Sower, Dymo Labeler
Rubber Stamps: MM Foam Stamps
Jigsaw Letters: Making Memories
Metal Tag:° K & Company

IDEA

The journaling inside the card reads: This little jar celebrates someone dear- YOU! If you will follow a simple plan, you will find that before this time next year you will have a very PERSONAL history finished! All you need to do is draw out one slip of paper each day (or at least once a week- it will just take longer to finish). On it you will find a question. Spend a few minutes and just enjoy remembering. Then paste the question in the journal at the top of the page and begin to write about it. Don't worry about spelling, handwriting, etc. Just tell YOUR story and remember you are loved!.

SUGGESTIONS TO BE USED IN MEMORY JAR.

Describe a favorite childhood friend and some things you did with him or her.

Describe getting a Christmas tree as a child, when did you put it up and decorate it?

Describe your first home as a young couple.

Did you and your father share an interest in any special activity?

Did you and your mother share an interest in any special activity?

Did you have a close relationship with any of your grandparents?

Do you like rainstorms? Why or why not?

Has anything major happened since the last time you wrote in this journal?

How did you become engaged?

How many are in your family? Do you wish you had more brothers and sisters?

Andrea's Planner

by Andrea Cloutier of Boca Raton, FL

Supplies:
Paper, Border Stickers and Letter Stickers: SEI, Sweetie Set
Stamp: Magenta
Ink: Tsukineko

Travel Journal

by Michaela Young Mitchell of Safford, AZ

Supplies:
Paper, Transparency, License Plate, Resin Letter, Stickers: Karen Foster
Fusible Fabric: Fast 2 Fuse
Cotton Twill Tape
Staples

TIP

I used the Fast 2 fuse for a light weight cover, but still made it sturdy enough for writing. The inside has sewn transparency pockets to store postcards, ticket stubs, receipts, and other keepsakes, and a sheaf of paper (5.5"x 8.5") for journaling notes and sketches.

Address Book

by Jeanne Wynhoff of Connell, WA

Supplies:
Ribbon: Fibers By the Yard
Patterned Paper: Mara-Mi Patterned Paper
Alphabet Stickers: Wordsworth

Stationery Folder

by Leigh King of Decatur, AL

Supplies:
Paper: Black Ink, Bazzill, Paper Reflections, me & my BIG ideas
White Cardstock
Ephemera: me & my BIG ideas, Paper Reflections
Stickers: Nostalgiques, Inspirables
Leaves: Black Ink
Stamps: Magenta, Rubber Stampede, Judikins, Stamp It, Stamp in the Hand, Stampabilities
Ink: Colorbox
Lacing Brad: Karen Foster
Other: Beads and Wire

IDEA

I made this Stationery Pocket Folder to hold handmade cards, dividing the pockets by month. A birthday/occasion /holiday list could be added to an inside cover with cards sorted accordingly. This folder could also be used to hold recipes, special notes, even bills or coupons. The pockets are created by folding a 12 x 12 piece of cardstock to create a 4" pocket. Fold this in half, creating a 6 x 8" page with a pocket on front and back. No adhesive is needed since you will bind the folder on the open sides of the pockets. Decorate with stamps, stickers and coordinating papers.

My School Stuff

by Tari Anderson of Vancouver, WA

Supplies:
Patterned Papers: Hot Off the Press
Label: Making Memories
Letter Stamps: Wordsworth
Ink: Ranger Industries
Ribbon: May Arts
Label Maker: Dymo
Cardstock: Provo Craft
Notebook: Mead

TIP
The base of this notebook is a composition book. I altered it by decorating it and adding tabs to the pages so it could be used for homework assignments.

Journal

by Leigh King of Decatur, AL

Supplies:
Paper: Paper Adventures, Li'l Davis, K & Company
Stickers: EK Success, Penny Black
Stamps: Making Memories, Post Modern Design, Hero Arts, Just For Fun
Fibers: Basic Grey
Ribbon: May Arts
Charms: EK Success, Darice
Other: Acrylic Paint, Postage Stamps, Composition Notebook

Memories Journal

by Catherine Allan of Twin Falls, ID

Supplies:

Patterned Paper, Epoxy Sticker: Rhonna Ferrer
Rub-Ons, Definitions: Making Memories
Charm: Embellish It
Keyhole, Watch Face and Handle: 7 Gypsies
Clip: Karen Foster
Ink: ColorBox Charcoal Chalk Ink

IDEA

I gave this to my mother and mother-in-law for their birthdays. The inside pocket has questions (i.e. What is your favorite color? What was Christmas like as a child? What was your bedroom like as a child?) for them to answer in journal form. It's my attempt to get family history information from them. I sewed patterned paper into pockets on the inside cover and decorated them. I also glued a ribbon to the back cover as a book mark.

Kathleen's Journal

by Kathleen Summers of Roseville, CA

Supplies:

Patterned Paper, Letter Rub Ons, Stickers: Wordsworth
Ribbon: Making Memories and Offray
Metal Photo Corners: Darice
Word Twill: Ribbon Expressions
Ric Rac: Adorned Pages.com
Mini Brads: Making Memories
Flower Punch: Paper Shapers

TIP

This was an inexpensive journal from Target with a design on the cover. The front cover is now completely redecorated.

Journal of Memories
by Jeanne Wynhoff of Connell, WA
Supplies:
Cardstock: Bazzill
Patterned Paper: Chatterbox
Spiral Binding: Office Depot
Ribbon: Fibers By the Yard
Circle Punch: Fiskars
Photo Turn, Mini Brad and Ribbon Charm: Making Memories
Label Maker: Dymo
Silk Flower
Stamp Ink: Memories

Randi's Notebook
by Randi Lanz of Attica, IN
Supplies:
Homework Paper: Doodlebug
Buttons, Twill: Junkitz
Cardstock: DMD
Double Sided Tape
Xacto Knife

A Circle Journal

by Kathleen Summers of Roseville, CA

Cover:
(I designed the background paper using cardstock, chalk, and a script stamp)
Patterned Paper - (diamond paper along spine): Provo Craft
Script Stamp - (to create background paper design): Limited Edition
Chalk: Craft-T Products
Ribbon: Offray
Fonts: P22 Garamouche and P22 Dearest
Embellished Frame: Donna Pittard

Sign-In Page:
The Sign In page is on the inside of the front cover. Each person creates a little tag to slide into her pocket.
Black Cardstock: National Cardstock
Vellum: unknown
Pocket Template: Deluxe Designs
Chalk: Craft-T Products
Letter Stamps: Hero Arts
Stamp Ink: StazOn
Embellished Tag: Donna Pittard

Cover Letter Page:
(Repeat of handmade background paper using cardstock and script stamp.)
Vellum
Chalk: Craft T Products
Font for letter: P22 Dearest Swash
Embellished Quote: Donna Pittard

IDEA

A group of friends each create a journal with their own theme and the journals is passed around in a "circle," each member of the group contributing their own page(s) to each journal. I covered a very inexpensive 3-ring binder designed to hold 4 1/4" x 5 1/2" pages, and created this in the landscape orientation.

Notes

by Jeanne Wynhoff of Connell, WA

Supplies:

Ribbon and Ric Rac: Fibers By the Yard

Cork Squarez: Lazer Letterz

Patterned Paper: Hot Off the Press

Buttons: Dress It Up

Charm: Unknown

Letter Stickers: Sonnets

Label Maker: Dymo

TIP

Be sure to sand the edges of your elements before inking. It makes the ink stick better and gives a more natural look.

Paris Journal

by Lara Gustafson of Glendale, AZ

Supplies:

Mini Journal: Magenta

Paper, Eiffel, P Block: Tim Holtz Distressables

Paris, Postcards: Tim Holtz

Ink Stewart Superior Palette Hybrid Inkpads

Do Not Disturb Door Hanger
by Melanie Douthit of West Monroe, LA
Supplies:
Patterned Papers: Flair Designs
Doorknob Hanger: Michaels
Rub-On Alphabets: Making Memories
Paint: Apple Barrell
Trim, Ribbon, Flowers: Hobby Store

Sara's Space
by Sara Bryans of Albany, NY
Supplies:
Paper: SEI Aunt Gerti's Garden
Rub-On Alphabets: Making Memories
Ribbon: Stampin' Up!
Ink Pad: Stampin' Up!
Brads: Lasting Impressions

Romance Door Hanger
by Sabrina Gould of Melbourne, FL
Supplies:
Door Hanger: Lara's Crafts
Cardstock: Bazzill
Patterned Paper: Daisy D's
Brads: Making Memories
Alpha Stamps: Hero Arts, Making Memories
Face Stamp: Hampton Arts
Ink: Ranger
Circle Clip: Making Memories
Silk Flower
Ribbon: Fiber By the Yard

Door Hangers can add a special touch to your home decor. Door Hangers are sometimes the first item noticed when entering a room. They can create a special anticipation to explore the room they introduce. A door hanger can introduce a theme of the room, or the style of person that lives within. Door Hangers can also be used for a specific purpose, for example, a locked or unlocked area, a non-smoking area, a sleeping baby, a dog warning or the reminder to be quiet. Use your imagination to create something different and create a door hanger for a special area.

Josh and Jake Door Hangers

by Pam Bumbaca of Litchfield, NH

Supplies:
Door Hangers: Craft Store
Acrylic Paint: Making Memories
Papers: Making Memories, Chatterbox
Oval Chipboard: Bazzill
Baseball: Fresh Cuts
Cork Letters: Lazer Letterz
Label Maker: Dymo
Ribbon: Adorned Pages and craft store
Slide Mount: Unknown
Flattened Bottlecap: Unknown
Letter Stickers: Unknown

Boys and Girls Hall Passes

by Susan Stringfellow of Cypress, TX

Supplies:
Patterned Cardstock: SEI
Stickers, Rub-On Words, Die Cuts: SEI
Ribbons and Sequin Trim on the girl pass: SEI
Ribbons and Ric Rac on the boy pass:
Fibers By the Yard
Buttons: SEI
Ink: Tsukineko
Bus and Globe Charms: Create a Craft
Letter Stamps: Rubber Stamp Ave
Wooden Door Hangers: Darice
Paint: Making Memories
Diamond Glaze: JudiKins
Modge Podge: Plaid

TIP

I made these for a friend of mine who will be teaching at an elementary school.

Dream Bookmark

by Carolyn Lontin
of Highlands Ranch, CO
Supplies:
White Linen Cardstock: Archiver
Ribbon: May Arts
Patterned Paper: KI
Circle Clip, Brad: Making Memories
Ink: Memories
Stamps: PSX
Paper Charms dream: Pebbles

My Girl

by Carolyn Lontin
of Highlands Ranch, CO
Supplies:
Patterned Papers: KI
Ribbons: May Arts
Flower Brads, Safety Pin: Making Memories
Tags: Office Depot
Stamps: Making Memories
Rub Ons: Scrapworks
Silk Flower
Brown Ink: Memories
Marisa Stamp: Stampendous

Friendship Bookmark

by Carolyn Lontin
of Highlands Ranch, CO
Supplies:
Patterned Paper: Chatterbox
Silk Flower
Brad, Ribbon: Making Memories
Zipper Pull: All My Memories
Friendship Rub-On: Unknown
Stamps: Making Memories

Creative bookmarks of today are not like the old bookmarks your grandmother used. Today, bookmarks can be personalized, detailed works of art. Pictures, embellishments and other memorabilia can be used to create unforgettable bookmarks. A personalized bookmark can be a wonderful gift for a special friend, or used for a special occasion. Imagine a special bookmark placed in the Bible used during a wedding or a surprise gift for the child beginning to read. Use your imagination and be creative. Bookmarks are little gifts that can make a big statement.

M Bookmark

by Carolyn Lontin
of Highlands Ranch, CO
Supplies:
Patterned Paper: American Crafts
Friendship, Twill: unknown
Silk flower
Zipper Pull: All My Memories
Brad: All Sorts of Things
"M" with Acrylic Paint:
Making Memories
Rub Ons: Doodlebug
Ribbon, Tags, Stamps,
Safety Pin: Making Memories

Father & Son Bookmark

by Carolyn Lontin of Highlands Ranch, CO
Supplies:
Cardstock: Archiver
Magic Mesh
Ribbon: May Arts
Brad: Making Memories
Photo Anchor: 7 Gypsies
Map Paper: unknown
Stamp: unknown
Ink: Memories

Imagine

by Carolyn Lontin
of Highlands Ranch, CO
Supplies:
Cardstock: Archiver
Patterned Paper: KI
Ribbons: unknown
Flower Brads, Magnetic Stamp:
Making Memories
Rub On: Scrapworks
"i" Sticker: American Crafts
Eyelet

Read Discover Learn

by Carolyn Lontin
of Highlands Ranch, CO
Supplies:
Cardstock: Archiver
Paper: Heidi Grace
Circle Clips: Making Memories
Ribbon: May Arts
White Gel Pen: American Crafts

Birthday Tags
by Cindy Harris of Modesto, CA
Supplies:
Party Hat Charm and Brad: The Happy Hammer
Large Round Eyelets: Stamp Dr.
Rub-On Letters: Making Memories
Colorful Birthday Cut-Outs: Puzzle Mates
Cardstock: Pebbles, Inc.
Black Ink: Stampendous
Other: Fiber

Birthday Wishes
by Leigh King of Decatur, AL
Paper, Monogram: Basic Grey
Stickers: Making Memories
Daisy Punch: EK Success
Accessories: Basic Grey, Bazzill

Tags have become an important part of scrapbooking and paper crafts. Tags can be used on a scrapbook page, a special gift, as an ornament, as an embellishment, and almost anything imaginable. Tags are mini works of art, so they can be used all over the house. You will see in this section, examples of tags being used as wall decor, invitations, journaling pieces, and gifts. Try your talent on tags and be surprised where your imagination can take you.

Happy Birthday Tag

by Teri Anderson of Idaho Falls, ID

Supplies
Patterned Paper: Anna Griffin
Ribbon: Making Memories, Offray
Rub-ons: Wordsworth, Doodlebug Design
Brad: All My Memories
Small Tags: 7Gypsies
Cake Sticker: Wordsworth
Black Pen: American Crafts

Happy Spring Tag

by Jeanne Wynhoff of Connell, WA

Ribbon: Fibers By the Yard
Cardstock: Bazzill Basics
Patterned Paper: Die Cuts With a View
Mini Brad: Die Cuts With a View
Word Stickers: Sticko, EK Success
Button: Junkitz
Eyelet Flower: Making Memories

IDEA
I made these as decorations to put on a shelf in a chid's room.

Girl/Boy Tag Signs

by Teri Anderson of Idaho Falls, ID

Supplies:
Patterned paper: All My Memories
Cardstock: DMD Industries, Bazzill Basics
Stamp ink: Ranger Industries
Cork and Cork Sliders: LazerLetterz (on boy's)
Transparency: Creative Imaginations (on girl's)
Brads and Foam Letter Stamps: Making Memories
Flower, Fish Die Cut: Quickutz
Spiral Clips: 7Gypsies
Ribbon: May Arts
Computer Font: Stamp Act
Other: Black Craft Paint

School Tag

by Leigh King of Decatur, AL

Paper: Bazzill, Karen Foster
Distressing Ink
Accessories: Karen Foster, Basic Grey
Ribbon: May Arts
Sticker: Bo-Bunny

School Tag

by Cindy Harris of Modesto, CA

Supplies:
Inspire Tag, Mini Safety Pin and Crayon Eyelet: The Happy Hammer
Ribbon: Queen & Co.
Cardstock: Bazzill
Patterned Paper: Pebbles, Inc.
School Cut-Outs: Embossible Designs
Alphabet Sticker("A"): Sticker Studio
Pen: American Crafts

TIP
I used a Slick Writer by American Crafts to carefully trace over the word Inspire on the metal tag to make it stand out.

BBQ Invitation

by Amy Brown of Eclectic, AL

Supplies:
Patterned Paper: Die Cuts With a View
Cardstock: Die Cuts With a View
Stickers: Karen Foster
Rub-On Letters: Making Memories
Rubber Stamps: Purple Onion Designs Garamouche
Ink: Making Memories

Bunco Tag

by Leigh King of Decatur, AL

Paper: Chatterbox
Ribbon: May Arts
Accessories: Deluxe Cuts, Quickutz. Karen Foster, Bazzill Buttons

Antique Tag
by Leigh King
of Decatur, AL
Paper: me & my BIG ideas
Accessories:
Paper Reflection, DMD
Ribbon

"L" Green & Blue Tag
by Carolyn Lontin
of Highlands Ranch, CO
Supplies:
Cardstock: Bazzill
Ribbon, Charm, Eyelet, L:
Making Memories
Words cut from
Club Scrap paint chips
Suede Square: unknown
Number Stamps: unknown

Pursuit of Happiness
by Carolyn Lontin
of Highlands Ranch, CO
Supplies:
Paper: Club Scrap
Circle Clip: Creative Impressions
"L" Eyelet: Making Memories
Eyelets
Stamps: Brother Sister Design Studio
Raffia: Club Scrap, Club Scrap
Number Stamps: unknown

Dragonfly Tag
by Carolyn Lontin
of Highlands Ranch, CO
Supplies:
Cardstock: Archiver
Patterned Paper: K & Company
Flower Snap: Chatterbox
Dragonflies: Jolee's Boutique
Number Stamps: unknown
Ribbon: Making Memories
L Sticker: Wordsworth
Black Ink: Memories

Grinning Kitty Halloween Treat Bucket
by Madeline Fox of River Ridge, LA
Supplies:
Patterned Paper: Scenic Route
Cardstock: Bazzill
Ribbons: Fibers By The Yard
Button: Junkitz
Page Pebbles: Making Memories
Paper Wire: unknown
Pen: Zig Writer
Paint Can: Home Depot

Halloween Pail
by Leigh King of Decatur, AL
Supplies:
Paper: Frances Meyer, Karen Foster
Stickers: Bo-Bunny
Accessories: Li'l Davis Designs, SEI
Ribbon: May Arts

Holidays can be the most memorable time of the year. Special handmade projects can make the season even more enjoyable. Whether it's spook-tacular Halloween ideas, fabulous Fall items or creative Christmas crafts, let your imagination spark a new idea and create something special for your home or a gift for someone special. For an added bonus to this Holiday section, you may want to review the other sections of this book to inspire a holiday idea. Use your imagination - the possibilities are endless!

Pumpkin Pals Tag
by Cindy Harris of Modesto, CA
Supplies:
Cardstock: DMD
Metal Frame: Making Memories
Paint Pen: Marvy
Ink: Tsukineko
Sticker: Phrase Cafe
Patterned Paper, Ribbon, Rick Rack, Patterned Brads and Photo Anchor: Queen & Co.

Happy Halloween Sign
by Jeanne Wynhoff of Connell, WA
Supplies:
Cardstock: Bazzill Basics
Patterned Paper: Paper Adventures
Stickers: Pebbles Inc
Wire: Artistic Wire
Fiber: Fibers By the Yard

Celebrate Halloween Tag
by Tristann Graves of Vancouver, WA
Supplies:
Cardstock: Bazzill
Ephemera Background Papers: Paper Pizazz, Hot Off the Press
Vintage Halloween Image: downloaded from internet
Transparency: Apollo
Ribbon: Offray
Web Button: unknown
Circle Alphabet Charm, Magnetic Stamp: Making Memories
Ink: Close to My Heart

Fall Tag
by Leigh King of Decatur, AL
Supplies:
Paper: Bo-Bunny
Stickers: me & my BIG ideas
Stamps: Rubber Stamp Tapestry
Accessories: Karen Foster, Junkitz
Raffia
Shipping Tag
Distressing Ink

Pumpkin Patch Tag
by Leigh King of Decatur, AL
Supplies:
Paper: Bo-Bunny, Frances Meyer
Sticker: Paper Bliss
Accessories: Li'l Davis, Bazzill, Karen Foster
Ribbon: May Arts

Hand Torn Pumpkin Tag
by Leigh King of Decatur, AL
Supplies:
Paper: Karen Foster
Corrugated Paper
Buttons
Wire Mesh
Twine

Fall Accordian Book

by Leigh King of Decatur, AL

Supplies:
Cover: Black Foam Board
Collage Paper, Tag in a Bag, Creative Tags: DMD and Paper Reflections
Letter Stickers: Fresh Cuts, EK Success
Charms: Embellish It
Domed, Torn Words, Black Label Words, Metal Art Frames: K & Co
Defined: Making Memories
Other: Metalic rub-Ons, Buttons, Twine, Snaps, Postage Stamps

Fall Decorative CD

by Jeanne Wynhoff of Connell, WA

Supplies:
Fiber: Fibers by the Yard
Cork Squarez: Lazer Letterz
Cardstock: Bazzill Basics
Patterned Paper: Daisy D's
Stickers: Snip Its and Colorbok
Ink: Colorbox Fluid Chalk

TIP
I drilled holes in the cd on the side to add the fiber.

Thanksgiving Decorative CD

by Susan Stringfellow of Cypress, TX

Supplies:
CD
Patterned Papers: Anna Griffin
Vintage Holiday Images Paper: Design Originals
Family Metal Tile: Kay
Cork Leaf: Lazerletterz
Beaded Trim: Walmart
Fibers: Fibers By the Yard
Brown Lace: Michaels
Letter Stamps: Rubber Stamp Avenue
Heart Button: Dress It Up
Silk Flowers: Artistic Silk
Antiqued Mini Brads: Making Memories
Ink: Ranger, Tsukineko
Corrugated Cardboard

IDEA
I recently received this promotional CD in the mail. The particule board case was so nice that I just had to alter it! I plan to use it to hold a cd of our holiday photos for this year, but I thought it would be a great holiday gift for family as well. Actually, it would work for any occasion or vacation where you could have many photos.

TIP
I texturized the surface with Texture magic dimensional paint, then painted it. The design is stamped with foam stamps and Acrylic Paint, then the words are stamped with Brown Stazon ink.

Christmas CD Case

by Susan Stringfellow of Cypress, TX

Supplies:
CD Case
Cardstock: Bazzill
Texture Magic Dimensional Paint: Plaid
Acrylic Paints: Delta
Large Decorative Foam Stamp: Making Memories
Letter Stamps: Rubber Stamp Avenue
Tiny Letter Stamps: Hero Arts
Small Flourish Stamp: Making Memories
Santa Image Transparency: Altered Pages
Believe Button: Dress it up
Decorative Molding: Making Memories
Fireplace Charm: Fibers By the Yard
Brown Ribbon: Hobby Lobby

Joy

by Sherry Wright of West Branch, MI

Supplies:
Three Match Boxes
Patterned Paper: Autumn Leaves
Ribbon: Offray
Trim: Wright's
Ink: Paper Salon
Three Bottlecaps
Gameboard Alphabet: Making Memories

Christmas Bag

by Carolyn Lontin of Highlands Ranch, CO

Supplies:
Gift Bag
Paper: Chatterbox, Petals & Possibilities
Stamps: Fontwerks
Sleigh charm: Making Memories
Tacks: Chatterbox
Magnetic Stamps: Making Memories
Ribbon: unknown

Christmas Gift Box

by Madeline Fox of River Ridge, LA

Supplies:
White Gable Box: Lifetime Moments
Patterned Papers: Flair Design and Carolee's Creations
Tag: Avery
Walnut Ink: Scraps of Time
Watercolors
Mulberry Leaves: Prima
Buttons: Junkitz
Fibers: Fibers By the Yard
Chalks: Craf-T Products

Holiday Greetings

by Tristann Graves of Vancouver, WA

Supplies:
Cardstock: Unknown
Green Tab and Envelope: Creek Bank Creations
Christmas Sticker Stack: Die Cuts With A View

Tis The Season Tag

by Tristann Graves of Vancouver, WA

Supplies:
Tag: Unknown
Paper: Hot Off the Press
Ribbon Words, Eyelet Charm: Making Memories
Photo Corners: Canson
Star Rhinestones: Decorative Details
Ruby Brads: Idea tool box
Ribbon: Offray

Wooden Christmas Ornament

by Susan Stringfellow of Cypress, TX

Supplies:
Wooden Tag: Limited Editions
Patterned Papers: SEI
Crochet Doilies: SEI
Ink: Stampin' Up
Ribbon: Offray
Fibers: Fibers By the Yard
Thread: Coats
Stamps: Hero Arts
Heart Brad: Accent Depot
Acrylic Paint: Plaid

Gingerbread Ornament

by Susan Stringfellow of Cypress, TX

Supplies:
Wooden Tag: Limited Editions
Patterned Paper: Die Cuts With a View
Acrylic Paints: Plaid
Crackle Medium: Plaid
Matte Mod Podge: Plaid
Gingerbread Man: Michaels
Polymer Clay: Sculpey
Ribbon: Michaels
Gold Cord: Crafts etc
Silk Poinsettia: Silk Impressions
Brass Mini Brad: Making Memories
Diamond Glaze: Judi Kins

TIP

Tip: The tag base is a wooden tag. I applied a coat of brown acrylic paint, a coat of Crackle medium, and a coat of beige acrylic paint. The patterned paper is decoupaged onto the tag using matte Mod Podge. The gingerbread man is a premade piece, but I made the "frosting" trim across the bottom using Sculpey polymer clay.

Joy Ornament

by Madeline Fox of River Ridge, LA

Supplies:
Jigsaw Alphabet (chipboard letter): Making Memories
Acrylic Paint: Plaid
Ribbon: Fibers By The Yard
Eyelet Word: Making Memories
Fabric: Junkitz
Jute

Angel Ornament

by Madeline Fox of River Ridge, LA

Supplies:
Jigsaw Alphabet (chipboard letter): Making Memories
Acrylic Paint and Crackle Medium: Plaid
Ribbon: Fibers By The Yard
Angel Button: JoAnne's
Gold Brads: Making Memories
Vellum: unknown

Happy Holidays Card
by Teri Anderson of Idaho Falls, ID
Supplies:
Tag Card: Making Memories
Happy Holidays Rub-ons: Making Memories
Snowflake Patterned Paper: Masterpiece Studios
Vellum: Provo Craft
Computer Font: 2Peas Jack Frost
Snowflake Punch: Marvy Uchida
Paper Clips: Acco
Ribbon: unknown

Let It Snow CD
by Jeanne Wynhoff of Connell, WA
Supplies:
Fiber and Ric Rac: Fibers By the Yard
Cork Letterz: Lazer Letterz
Patterned Paper: NRN Designs
Snowflake Jewels: Unknown
Metal Tag: Diecuts With a View
Mini Brads: Diecuts With a View
Stickers: Bo-Bunny
Word Stickers: EK Success
Paint Pen

Star Gift Box
by Madeline Fox of River Ridge, LA
Supplies:
White Petal Box: Lifetime Moments
Ink: Tim Holtz, Ranger
Leafing Pen: Krylon
Star Stamp: Great Impressions
Embossing Liquid: Stampcraft
Embossing Powder: Stampendous
Fibers: Fibers By The Yard

INDEX BY THEME

INDEX BY PRODUCTS & TECHNIQUES